The Story of Your Life

Write Your Own Obituary

By
Charlie Seraphin

ANGEL
MOUNTAIN
PUBLISHING

Angel Mountain Publishing, First Edition, October 2023

ISBN: 978-1-7377731-3-9

Website: CharlieSeraphin.com

Cover Art: Adobe Stock

"In a little while the world will no longer see me, but you will see me, because I live and you will live."

(John 14:19)

Table of Contents

Introduction

You Know You Best

More important than all the selfies in your photo file, your obituary captures the essence of your life. Unfortunately, if you don't write it yourself, it won't get done properly.

That's what happened to my dad. Here's my dad's obituary, taken from the Rhinelander Daily News in April, 1962:

Joseph Seraphin Dies Here Today

Joseph Arthur Seraphin, 68. A lifelong resident of Rhinelander died in St. Mary's Hospital this morning after an extended illness. He lived at 35 Lake Creek Rd. and operated the Lake Creek Grocery store the last 10 years. Born here on Jan. 20, 1894, Mr. Seraphin operated a tavern for many years.

He is survived by his wife, Betty: four sons, John, Charles, Michael and Mark, all at home; a daughter, Miss Mary Catherine Seraphin of Milwaukee, and a sister, Mrs. Raymond Powers of Rhinelander.

Services will be held at 9 a.m. Wednesday in St. Joseph's Church, officiated by the Rev. Joseph Miller. Burial will be in St. Joseph's Cemetery. After 2p.m. Monday the body will be in the Hildebrand Funeral Home. The rosary will be said at 8 p.m. Monday.

If you knew my dad, you'd laugh at how little he resembled the person described here. My dad was a bootlegger; he spent 18 months in federal penitentiary for operating an unlicensed still after prohibition in 1932. His still was the largest ever confiscated by federal officials in the northwoods. He took the fall for his crew operating the still because the others had children and, at the time, he did not. He was also the operator of a brothel and a couple speakeasies. He did run a grocery store as described in this obituary, but he was also a boxer, an inventor, a farmer, and an expert horse trainer. His published obituary says nothing about character, values, beliefs, idiosyncrasies, hobbies, skills, or anything else that explains who he was.

If you search the archives for my father's obituary, you'll find it under Joseph. Nobody ever called him Joseph either. His name was Joe. The obituary also referred to me as Charles. Nobody ever called me Charles. My name is Charlie. Maybe it's not a big deal, but when your obituary calls you and your offspring by names they never use, your life story is anything but accurate. Don't allow your obituary to be written by someone who doesn't know you or your life.

At this point you might be asking: Why should I care about my obituary? I'm not dead or dying. I'm in the prime of my life. I can't even see the end from here. Exactly. That's why you need to write your own obituary today. If you wait until you're dying, you'll be distracted. Don't let a stranger write the story of your life. Do it now, while you still remember your life clearly. But there's an even more important reason: Reviewing your life, at every stage, helps you figure out where you've been, where you are, and where you're going. Remembering people and events from your past, brings the present into focus. If you end up with a well written obituary, that is a bonus.

A few years ago, my friend John emailed an obituary written by his father-in-law. It was a wonderful document written by a man named Mike. He used wit, humor, and self-deprecation. He cited his quirks and foibles to tell the story of his life. He had a unique and brilliant way of sharing his story. He did it in his own words, in his own time.

When he wrote his obituary, he wasn't sick or feeling terminal. It would be ten years before he died. Nonetheless he set out to describe a great life. A few years after writing his obituary he developed Alzheimer's. As the end of his life approached, his cognitive ability abandoned him, and he was unable to write. If he hadn't written his obituary long before he died, his memories would have been lost forever. Fortunately, Mike's wit and humor live on:

3

"He did not pass away or begin a new journey. He did not get called home to his Heavenly Father or his Lord of Love, or set off to attain eternal rest. He did not ascend to heaven in the Lord's hands. He did not battle bravely. He just died. For those close to him and concerned about his legacy, he will be remembered as a warm, loving, sensitive, caring, happy, multi-pseudonymous, man. Mike, honest to a fault, would approve only that part of his legacy that made it known to the world that he made it known to the world that he liked to use pseudonyms."

Nobody could have told his story better than him. What a guy. What a great idea. There has never been anyone exactly like you or Mike. He inspired this book. His commitment to accurately recording his life is more than inspirational, it's something that every one of us can and should do.

While you are alive and healthy is the only time you will have to get your affairs in order. ***The Story of Your Life*** is about making the most of the time you have left, by recalling the past, sharing your most important memories, and expressing what's on your mind today. Facts (data points) don't tell us anything about you. Many people were born where you were born, lived where you lived, and died where you died. None of them have your memories. Here's your chance to keep those memories alive.

Regardless of what you believe, death is the biggest transition you'll ever make. Everyone dies. One minute you're living and the next you're not. Most of us cherish religious traditions and faith, without physical proof of what happens next. Scholarly studies about death take us up to the line, but that's where the science ends.

Believers and non-believers see death differently. Faith inspires confidence without hard evidence. Lack of faith often fosters intense fear of death. You may have a precise idea of what heaven is like. It may come from scripture or religious education. Some have suggested that hell resembles our worst days on earth. Whatever waits for us on the other side, it's certain that when we get to our final destination, we'll be amazed and astounded, even if it doesn't resemble what we pictured.

Being forgotten is one reason people fear death. On earth, most of us will be forgotten in two generations or less. We might remember our grandparents, but our recollection of great-grandparents or relatives that came before them is marginal. If we simply live, die, and are gone; then life is meaningless. If we are spiritual beings with eternal souls, then death is just an event along a continuum. Collecting and sharing memories from your life is meaningful now—and even more so after you're gone.

I have read and continue to read obituaries. The one constant is that they rarely tell us the most important things about the person who died. They feature basic facts like when and where a person was born, who they left behind, where they worked, and a few random details. Rarely does an obituary tell us anything about who the person truly was, or more importantly *why* they were *who* they were.

How will you be remembered? Will your obituary list a few unrelated facts, or will it include your authentic, fun-filled narration? How different life would be if deceased loved ones had left more colorful descriptions. What they believed and why they believed what they did. What they experienced and how it impacted them. How they felt about significant issues. How they came to terms with their regrets. Those kinds of recollections are powerful. Isn't that what we want to know when we search for information about other people?

How about you? How often do you ask yourself those questions? How much time do you devote to reviewing things that happened during your life? There's instant value in reflection and remembering. Can you explain what you believe and why or how you came to be the way you are? Probably not off the top of your head. You'd have to think about it. That's what this exercise is about—examining our past in order to live better today.

Digital technology allows us to preserve our memories forever. Once positioned in the digital cloud, your obituary lasts indefinitely. Since in today's world virtually all recorded information is preserved, once you hit the save key, you can rest assured that the memories you save won't be forgotten. Regardless of your attitude about life, death, or life after death, whether you live to be a hundred or die next year, preserving your personal footprint is as important as anything you can do.

Creating a record of your life has many benefits. No two people are the same. Nobody knows you and your story as well as you. Nobody cares about you as much as you do. Nobody is more qualified to document your story. And if you don't do it, there's no telling who will, but odds are, they'll make mistakes.

Setting aside the time to tell your story is important. Until now, there hasn't been an easy guide for organizing and laying out your life experiences, your values, what you believe, and why you believe it. Sharing your experiences benefits both you and those you love. That's what we're doing here.

Throughout this book, I'm going to ask you to recall every significant person and event in your life. I'll make it easy by asking specific questions to prompt you. Once you get the hang of it, you'll begin to recall things that may have escaped your memory. Then we'll cull those memories until you have a document that represents exactly what you want to say.

What you choose to include in your obituary is personal and private. Separate the weeds from the crop, the important from the mundane, the worth sharing from the insignificant. Even if your memory isn't the greatest, the questions will unlock secret passages in your brain. Your personal interests, passions and values will rise to the top. Those are most important. Your job, your hobbies, and your passing fancies can be interesting, but as you weigh one memory against the next, you'll have to decide what's included and what is left out. Perhaps the most challenging questions are: "Why are you here?" and "What are you willing to share about your life?"

From the beginning until now, we'll examine many aspects of your life. As you remember, you'll learn things about yourself that transcend data. Most obituaries only contain data points. Born, died, left behind, jobs, hobbies, interests. Great obituaries explain what you've done, why you did it, and what the impact was on others. Anybody can spit out facts. Only you can capture your significant memories, the essence of your life.

As you go through the chapters of this book, you'll see many options. Some subjects are important to you, others are not. Your obituary should come together like a buffet at a cafeteria. You get to pick which sections are important, and which you'd rather not include. No section is required. You can add and subtract as we get further into the process. You set the record straight and tell your story the way you want it told. Even if some people don't like the way you say it, they'll appreciate that you were honest, direct, and forthright.

The words you choose to tell your story are powerful. Your obituary will include details that only you can recollect. By following the prompts anybody can create an "eternal record." Each chapter focuses on an aspect of your life. Some of the suggestions will seem important, others may not. These questions are designed to prompt you to reflect upon your life and how you want to be remembered. Since you are one of a kind, your obituary will be unique.

As you begin reflecting on the people, places, and events in your life, you'll likely find some problem areas. Life is like a jigsaw puzzle. If you only concentrate on one piece, the one in your hand today, you may never solve the puzzle. Sometimes that piece just doesn't fit. Step back and take a look at the big picture. Today's problem might be something that happened a long time ago. In puzzles and life, if you can't find the problem, the picture is never quite right.

Notes

1

What Do You Remember Most?

Your life is important. It matters. It is filled with meaning, memories, adventures, and experiences. Letting life pass without recording some highlights is wasteful. Record your accomplishments. Admit your failures and shortcomings. Clear the air.

Remembering your stories is easy and fun. As you go through the process, you'll laugh and be inspired. You may shed a tear. Remembering shines a new light on elements of your life you've long forgotten. And as you remember, you may even decide to make adjustments. Mistakes can be corrected. Wounds can be healed. Lessons can be shared. Organizing and sharing your stories is bound to improve the way you treat yourself and others. Pull back the curtain and take an honest look at your past.

Thanks to modern technology, you have the opportunity to touch and influence someone who is yet to be born. Your life stories will reside in a virtual time capsule called the internet. Between now and the foreseeable future, anyone who searches your name will find you. Everyone who comes looking will have access to your story. So why not make sure it's written in your own words?

Life involves a series of choices. An examination of what we thought, said, did, and believed in the past, creates opportunities for behavioral modification in the present. For example: You will feel differently about death after you finish reading this book. If you're fearful now, odds are good you'll be less fearful. Remembering the events that made you who you are helps make your life—and especially your childhood—easier to understand. Depending on what happened in your past, you'll either be more or less judgmental tomorrow.

The process of reflecting and sharing memories adds perspective. Perspective adds clarity. When you consciously take time to consider important people and events in your life, it changes everything. There are so many details that have been forgotten or pushed to the back of our memory. Digging into those details leads to "ah ha" moments.

Sometimes when you can't figure out where you're going, the best way to find your way is to consciously remember where you've been. You can't appreciate all the special moments you've experienced until you remember them. You've done more, accomplished more, influenced more, and inspired more than you might think. By sharing those private memories, you multiply the odds that they will be remembered.

Consciously or unconsciously, we put a lot of energy into cultivating a public image. Some of us spend considerable time in front of a mirror wondering what others see when they see us. We apply makeup and dress for success (whatever that means), and we work to project an image that we imagine to be attractive. The result is often a distorted public image, too often one that bears little resemblance to who we really are.

My previous book, ***When Did You Stop Being You: In Search of Your Personal Brand***, details this process. The problem stems from the fact that public images are often based on desired results rather than truth. We want to be liked, and we get trapped in the cycle of pretending. Lies beget lies. Public images, propagated for decades, contain false information, based on false narratives.

The problem is exacerbated by social media. The internet is full of false information. Google yourself and see if your online profile tells your story accurately. That's why your obituary needs to be written by you ahead of time, with your stamp of personal approval. Your authentic statements will include information about thoughts, words, beliefs, and values that can't be found in other sources. Without them, your online record is incomplete, or possibly even fake.

Digital changes the game when it comes to preserving recorded legacy. In the digital world, virtually all recorded information is preserved. As soon as you hit the save key, what you wrote is locked in a virtual time vault. Thus, once in the digital cloud, your obituary will be preserved indefinitely. It is a form of eternal, even for those who don't believe in eternal.

When someone in the future downloads your story, they'll find just what you recorded, in your own words. Regardless of your attitudes about life and death, what other people think about you, whether you live to be a hundred or you die next year, your recollections are preserved.

You can't fix problems until you acknowledge them. Reviewing your life gives you the opportunity to do just that. That doesn't mean you'll be saved in a spiritual sense. Your obituary isn't a promise of eternal happiness, but what you write is saved. And if you're honest about what you share, your chances to be saved in a spiritual sense will soar.

The process of peeling back each chapter of your life, will help you develop insights that you can't even imagine. One memory ties to another and recalling significant milestones uncovers new meanings related to old events. As you engage in self-reflection and self-improvement, you'll discover things about yourself that you've forgotten, both good and bad.

When you consider all the things that occupy our time—reading, television, social media, social events, hobbies, vegging, etc.—it's hard to argue that any of these is more important than preserving an honest record of our life. Death lasts a long time. Setting aside a few minutes to tell your story is one of the more meaningful things you can do. If you share the process with loved ones, they are likely to recommend stories you should include. "Don't forget to tell about the time…" If you include others in the process, they'll help you remember things that may not be top of mind.

Every time you recall special moments you come away with fresh perspectives. You ask yourself questions like: "Why did I do that?" and "What was I thinking?" Those answers create valuable insights that you may have missed way back then. It's that convergence of past life story and current day interpretation that make your obituary a powerful document for you and anyone who reads it.

Getting Started

Remember when epitaphs appeared on headstones in the cemetery? Since not many people get buried in cemeteries these days, you might instead think of it as the title of your eternal web page. In contemporary terms, it's your hashtag, your personal brand. It's a summary description of yourself…in the past tense. And for the purpose of this exercise, it's how we begin. The first line of your obituary sets the tone for everything that follows.

Your obituary should start with a sentence or phrase that summarizes how you want to be remembered. Here are some examples:

- "Intense, spiritual, quirky."
- "Father, Friend, Funny."
- "He was a good man."
- "She was a woman of conscience."
- "Totally committed father."
- "Mama told me not to come."
- "Super mom."
- "A lover, not a fighter."
- "Fearless in life."
- "Loyal to the core."
- "Beer and barbeque."
- "Always climbed back up."
- "Thoughtful to a fault."
- "Broke every glass ceiling."

I recommend that you write in the third person. There are a

number of benefits, not the least of which is that you can have more fun talking about yourself when you write about yourself in the third person past tense. Mike's obituary in the introduction illustrates this point.

What do people always say about you? Is it true? Do you have a handle? A professional name? An alias? Are you serious or silly? Are you secular or religious? Skinny or fat, short or tall? Is there any one expression that people use to describe you when you're not around? Did your mother give you a nickname that stuck with you for the rest of your life? Jot down the first ones that come to mind. If you aren't sold on your epitaph today, you can change it when you come up with a better phrase.

If you are a person of faith you may want to include a deeply held belief in your summary statement:

- "She's Gone Home to Jesus."

Athletes can include a sports metaphor:
- "He Skipped Into The Endzone."

There are no bounds here:
- "She loved more than a dozen men." (that one would attract some attention)

- "He hated all his patients." (Does that remind you of any of your doctors?)

For those who think life is boring, dig a little deeper. You are unique. There's something you know that nobody else knows. You've experienced things that no one can even imagine. Take time to reflect. There's a line in there that will set you apart:

- "He Turned Down a Ride on a UFO." (Remember him?)
- "Cosmic Lady–A Woman of the Universe" (She was a San Francisco icon.)

Take something from your past—"He Had Beautiful Baby Teeth"—or something more contemporary—"Adult Braces Gave Her Confidence."

Humor works, but not for everyone. You might try asking a few close friends to describe you in a few words (that's always interesting), but at the end of the day (literally) it's your story and you can tell it any way you see fit. As we go along, and you answer more questions about yourself, you may come up with an entirely different approach. For now, write down a couple words and move on.

How you describe yourself says a lot about who you are. People often struggle with self-description. It's hard to separate who we are from how we're perceived. Some people will be surprised by your epitaph. They see you very differently than how you see yourself. If your epitaph is a grabber, you'll generate more interest. If you're exceptionally creative, your obituary could go viral. You'll still be dead, but wouldn't it be something to be more famous in death than in life? People will say, "I never knew this person, but I wish I had."

If you go with the "down home" or humorous approach, it will be obvious that you value having fun. If you're more cerebral, your summary statement will probably contain some esoteric clues about your character. Since not everybody gets you in this life, it's likely that not everybody will get you when you're gone.

There are an infinite number of ways to approach your summary statement/epitaph. Your epitaph is whatever you want it to be, serious, fun, silly, thoughtful, or challenging. Don't be concerned with how many times you change your epitaph. This is a dynamic exercise. Your story changes from day to day. Some days are better than others. Some experiences are more impactful. Don't stress over it now, simply jot down ideas as they come to you, and try to find one that you think will stand the test of time.

Who Are You Writing For?

Remember that your obituary is a draft of history. Nobody has ever told your story the way you're about to tell it. What you create will become the eternal record of your life (at least as far as earthly historical records). Regardless of what anybody else says about you, your obituary is the last word. Written by you, in your voice, it becomes the only insight into how you approached life. Who you are in your obituary is who you are. Whether it is a legal document, or something intended only for close friends and family, there will be no question about what you deemed most important. A well-crafted obituary stands the test of time.

As you start to write the story of your life, you'll have to decide whether you want to write for multiple audiences (haters, lovers, strangers), or if you have a particular audience in mind (family and close friends). Writing for a broad audience means a little more thought and a bit more work. Writing for your immediate family is easier. Even so, this isn't paint by number. Each obituary is completely different. When you finish, regardless of what you share or how you share it, your obituary will stand alone.

You can pick any style and write it however you like. Personal letters written to a single person often serve as obituaries. Whether you make an intimate statement, or a broadcast announcement, is entirely up to you.

What's your story? What do you remember that you don't often talk about? What do you remember from your childhood that upon reflection seems totally random? What did you see or do that you haven't thought about in years. Why is it significant? How did it change your outlook?

Have fun. Remembering takes you from the significant to the insignificant. Your "life changing event" can be as embarrassing as drinking too much and vomiting. Ever done that? Or, it can be breath-taking, like the time you saw a UFO.

Writing your obituary isn't just a statement of facts. This is a reconstruction project. An opportunity to share…good and bad. As you reflect and remember, relive experiences, and focus on valuable life lessons, you gain new insights into yourself. When you share your experiences, the ones that are significant or zany, they become gifts to future generations. You'll be gone, but your recollection of special experiences and the lessons they taught will live on.

Once you delve into your memory banks, odds are you'll remember a lot more than you care to share. Try to share examples that demonstrate your values and priorities.

Even when you're not writing your obituary, it's healthy to spend time remembering every day. A few minutes in the morning or at night before you go to sleep will help you peel back the layers of your life. Self-discovery is a process. It may be a little scary at first, but the more you know about yourself, the more you can take control of your thoughts, words and actions in real time.

Reflection
"Read an obituary, then ask yourself what you really know about the person who died."

Notes

2

Where Did You Come From?

The details of when and where a person was born are included in almost every obituary. Why does it matter? Where you were born is a very special piece of information. You don't have to be proud of where you were born. After all, you had no control over that. Many people were born somewhere and moved elsewhere as babies or young children. But where you were born has had an effect on your life.

People who don't know where they were born are rarer than people who don't know their parents. What was the date? Most people include when and where details, but you don't have to. Do you know any more about your birth? Were there unusual circumstances? Were you born in the back seat of a Greyhound bus rolling down Highway 41?

Many of our ancestors lived in the same location for their entire lives. Most of us have moved, at least once. Whether you've moved more than twenty times, lived in Europe, Asia or Africa for a couple years, and settled in a place far from where you were born…or if you and your ancestors always lived in the same town, it's part of your story.

25

You may not remember all the details of some of your life adventures, but simply inserting a couple short sentences paints a picture. If your story is not about places you lived, it might be about some of the people who live in those places. Think of your geography as a multifaceted plant with roots, branches, and buds. Include the information that feels significant.

There are places on the globe and times in your life that resonate more than others. Maybe it's a place you lived briefly. Maybe you lived there all your life. Perhaps it's a place you never visited, but wish you had. Maybe you were born there and have only fleeting memories. Whatever the specifics, places are either important or unimportant depending on the value you ascribe to them. It's your life sketch. For now, just write down the names of some cities, towns, and geographic areas. Once you get into the rhythm of writing your obituary, you'll know which stories should be included and how much detail to include.

Oftentimes places connect to important life events. You may have only been there once, but it's where you met the love of your life. You saw a house that you admired when you were on a trip and spent the next ten years trying to build that house somewhere else. Connecting people, places and things is fun. As you go down this road, you'll remember details that will help explain some of your likes and dislikes. If you had a bad experience in a particular location, you probably don't have a desire to return. That story might explain some facet of your character.

Try to remember specific physical structures, a doorway, a kitchen or bedroom, a house you lived in or walked by. We all have memories associated with specific places and structures. Remembering places brings you a step closer to remembering who you were when you were there.

As we change and grow, sometimes our brightest days seem behind us. For the purpose of writing your obituary, your past and your future are inexorably linked to today. What you choose to remember, the decisions you made, what you planned, and what you share are all important. They are the cornerstones of this project.

Childhood

Your core values may come from where you grew up. People from cities are different from folks who grew up in rural areas. Locations have socio-economic stigmas. If you grew up in a rich neighborhood there may have been constant pressure to compete. If you lived in a poor neighborhood, nobody paid much attention to what you didn't have. People, places and things. Where you were born, where you were raised, and where you live say a lot about who you are. You're describing the places you lived and how they impacted your formation. Your words are sure to enlighten future generations.

Is there a takeaway from your childhood neighborhood? How did it shape your world? Did you shake off the chains and leave your past behind? Do you cherish every moment of your early years? Life adventures all have beginnings. Whether you embrace or reject yours says a lot about who you are today. Remember, your goal is to explain who you are. Where you came from is part of that explanation.

Everyone had a childhood, but some were more pleasant than others. What do you remember about yours? Did you have a traditional family? Were you raised by someone other than your natural parents? Did you suffer any early childhood diseases or illness that affected your life? Did you get a good education? Do you remember any of your grade school teachers or classmates? Which ones? Why do you remember them?

Describe your childhood in a sentence or two, or tell a couple stories about your earliest adventures. Sometimes our childhood stories aren't really our memories, but memories derived from hearing our parents or others relate those stories. Your sister or brother may tell a story about you before you were old enough to remember. You may have photographs from your childhood with people and places you don't actually recall. Anything that sparks a memory is fair game, and you can spend as much time remembering your childhood as you deem necessary.

We've all met people whose childhood was the pinnacle. Child movie stars come to mind. Your parents may have moved you to or from a foreign country at a young age. That was sure to have created an interesting reflection or two.

For others, childhood was such a long time ago that it doesn't seem that important. But, if you're going for context and perspective, there's probably at least one incident that deserves note. Don't worry about the people who affected your life as a child. We'll deal with them in another section. This is just about you and your recollections of life as a child.

Do you have childhood friends that you keep in contact with? What kinds of things did you enjoy as a child? Did you have disappointments? Can you remember your happiest times? Who and what were involved?

This section requires a trip down memory lane, the first of many we'll cover in your obituary. For some, an uneventful childhood is what it is. If you can't think of anything special about the time you spent growing up, try to reach back into those memory cells and drag up a few happy and a few sad recollections. Did something happen that changed the direction of your life? A move? A birth? A death? If not, or if you prefer not to say, you can skip this section.

Family

The family section of any obituary is challenging. You may want to start, think about each relationship, and then come back and finish the family section later. If you didn't get along with your parents, or your children didn't turn out the way you hoped, don't be too hard on them or yourself. Remember, there has never been a foolproof way to raise perfect children. Raising a child is mostly trial and error.

For most of us, family plays a critical role in our story. Unfortunately, most obituaries list names without explaining connection. That's where your obituary is different. Instead of listing names and biological connections, you can share information in greater depth. You'll be writing about who they are and why they're important.

Consider one of those movies where the executor of the estate reads the last will and testament before a packed room of greedy relatives. In those movies, the person least likely to get anything, gets everything, and the snotty heirs who expect to inherit the estate are left with a bar of soap. (I love those movies.)

In a very real sense, what you're doing in your obituary is sending a message from the grave. If that sounds macabre to you, you're not paying attention. This is a cathartic exercise. It's the ultimate stress release. When you finish writing your obituary, you don't have to worry about anything else. And, as long as you're still alive, you can always change the narrative to incorporate new elements and make the story of your life what you want it to be.

Most obituaries contain some information about parents, siblings, and children. What can you share about yours? If you remember grandparents, there may be something special you'd like to share about them as well. Just a sentence or two can paint an incredible picture. Were you close to your parents? Were they special people? Were you raised by grandparents or another relative? Give them their due.

What about your siblings? Were you closer to one than another? Have you considered why? Does it deserve mentioning, or do you prefer to leave the past in the past?

Note: Please consider privacy. If you are going to write things that you don't want released prematurely, make plans to keep your obituary in a secure file or under lock and key. If you're not worried about hurting anyone's feelings, simply make it a working document on your computer.

The most important thing to consider is honesty. Here's your chance to tell your aunt how much you appreciated her, or your brother that he regularly disappointed you. The goal isn't to create ill will, but it's your legacy, and you can elevate and diminish as you see fit. Whether you include information or leave it out, please don't sugarcoat. Don't go out of your way to hurt someone's feelings, but balance that against being honest. As your mother may have told you: "If you can't say something nice, don't say anything at all."

Start with those who had a significant effect on your life. If it's your parents, grandparents, spouse or children, go ahead and tell them how you feel about them and why. Try to remember specific examples of times when they said or did something that touched your heart (or upset you).

If you were molested by your grandfather or if you had some other horrible family experience, writing it here might help others understand you better. If you have the courage, bare your soul and clear the air. Remember, you might be dead by the time your obituary is published, so you can set the record straight without fear of reprisal or recrimination. For some of you, it may be the only time you get the last word.

Don't rush. Take your time. Think about it. Upon reflection, you might decide that some of your relatives are just genetic connections. They don't mean a lot to you in life, so you don't have to build them up in death. Others were game-changers. They taught you things that you never forgot. They literally changed your life. Why not give them a solid plug? You don't have to mention everyone. Think it through, but don't stress over it. People you leave out may feel slighted. It's better to concentrate on your message than worry about how your message may be interpreted.

In that imaginary crowded room at your celebration of life, everyone is waiting to hear what you have to say. Your mission is to tell the truth. As your obituary is read, the crowd may erupt in shouts of joy, or your words may suck the air out of the room. Your obituary. Your choice.

Don't forget to factor in generational evolution. Your family story has evolved over the years. You're different from your grandparents, and your world is radically different from your great-grandparents' world. The world and the families that live in it are constantly evolving. What you share will be read by people who aren't born yet. They will have a different perspective. You might have to explain some things about your life and put them in context in order to communicate meaning. On the other hand, you're welcome to say whatever you like, any way you want to say it, with or without regard for future generations.

Do you want to say something about anyone who preceded you in death? What was their impact on your life? Your grandchildren? Is there a lesson you'd like to share with them? If you're not sure who to include, take a page from a traditional obituary. Who would be listed as your survivors? If you choose, you can give them recognition. Or, you can intentionally leave them out.

It might help to make a simple genealogy chart. You can go back as far as you deem necessary. The goal is to tell YOUR story, so if they provided influence in your life, explain how. If not, you have the choice of mentioning them or not. Are your family members interesting, good people, bright, and capable? Let them know.

Inspirational People

We've all been blessed to meet inspirational people. As time passes, we often forget them and the impact they had on our life. If you've already shared inspirational stories about relatives, you might want to use this space to write about someone outside your family that changed your life.

Many of us were inspired by teachers. Do you remember one that taught you a particularly important life lesson? Did you ever have a boss that you felt "hung the moon?" Did a friend or neighbor change the way you look at things or teach you a valuable lesson or skill? Was there a pastor who brought a clearer understanding of scripture?

Is there someone who stands out because of their kindness, empathetic attitude, or authentic friendliness? Some people are prone to mention celebrities they met in passing. Careers, creativity, and accomplishments are important, but they pale in comparison to the impact of authentic human interaction. As you set out to write your story, remember that fame and fortune are interesting, but personal values and the lessons they teach are your treasured characteristics.

Good people accomplish great things. Think about the people you've inspired and those who have inspired you. Those are the obituary stories that will set the bar for your life. When you remember influential people in your life, think of them in terms of their character. This section tells a lot about you. Your heroes, the people you look up to, say everything about who you are.

As you review your life, and remember people that inspired you, ask yourself what it was about them that made them special. Whether you write their names in your obituary or just share their stories, remembering people and their impact helps clarify who you are. If we existed in isolation, if we were self-made automatons, we wouldn't mention anyone else in our obituary. But if you are honest about it, there were many people along the way that helped you develop into the person you are today.

Giving credit and a nod of thanks is a way of demonstrating to future generations the importance of human relationships. The people you choose to remember had an impact on you. What you do has an impact on people in your world. Your obituary, especially this section, can influence inhabitants of the future. Sharing stories of appreciation perpetuates the "pay it forward" process. Pulling one another up through demonstrated values is powerful. Being influenced and influencing others is essential.

Even if you don't include their names in your obituary, a stroll down memory lane to identify the people who inspired you has benefits. Write down their names. What did they do to or for you? If you're like me, there are many. When we were down, someone was there to lift us up. It happens in every life story. Whether you include them is your choice, but simply remembering them helps make your life richer. You can always come back and add to this or other sections of your obituary as you continue the remembering process.

Reflection
"Are you being honest, or spinning the same stories that you've been telling for years?"

Notes

3

What Have You Accomplished?

In death, as in life, the important things have more to do with the heart than with bank statements. Truly creative people create. They invent or shine a light on things that were previously unseen or ignored. If you're one of those people, state your accomplishments. If not, there are plenty of other areas of your life that define you.

What were you passionate about? Did you help others achieve their goals? Were you a mentor? Did you make your first million before you were twenty-one and donate half the money to the poor? Did you inspire others to follow in your footsteps?

The mosaic of your life is filled with colorful people and events. Spending time doing something doesn't make it important. For example: We spend considerable time sleeping, but your obituary can do without a sleep description. If, however, a daily nap is part of your routine, that says something about you too. It's your choice whether or not naptime is important enough to mention in your obituary.

Work

Whether you think of it as a job or a career, for purposes of writing your obituary we'll call it work. Work is one part of this story, but most jobs don't define who we are. Even though you've "worked hard" all your life, and spent most of your time on the job, for many of us, work doesn't rank among our most important achievements. More than anything, your obituary should be a <u>reflection of your values</u>. If it's important to you, it belongs in the story. If it demonstrates how you react under pressure, or how you apply personal values to work situations, by all means tell the story.

A lot of people think work is the most important element in their life. On the other hand, nobody will miss it if you leave this section out. I've read obituaries that detail every title, company, and minor employment achievement. He or she was a great clerk, an accomplished high school coach, or a dependable plumber. Is that all you have to say? Jesus was a carpenter. When we tell his story, how much do we focus on his job? It was a job. It provided income. He made things with his hands, but in the grand scheme of things, his carpentry had little to do with his legacy. Who he was, not what he did for a living, captured the imagination of millions over centuries.

Your work took a lot of your time, but only you can

decide whether it is a defining factor. It might help people place you in space and time, but your work is less important than who you are. Obituaries that read like resumes tell us little or nothing about a person. If work is the only way you've defined your success until now, it's time for some honest reflection. Here are the pertinent questions:

- Did your job performance change lives for the better?
- Did you provide inspiration to superiors and subordinates?
- Did your co-workers (Jesus forgive me) worship the ground you walked on?

If so, by all means, share the details. We can all learn and benefit from greatness. Do fancy titles and high incomes say anything about a person's character or who they are? A hundred years from now many titles and job descriptions will no longer exist. It's entirely possible that what today we consider meaningful work will come off as blah, blah, blah.

The effort you put into improving the lives of others is eternal. Your role as a mother, father, neighbor, or friend will be remembered. Famous people who made lots of money like movie and sports stars are normally remembered online. Unfortunately, many of the books written about famous people describe lonely, dispassionate, selfish individuals. Too few of the rich and famous leave legacies of love and compassion. Your obituary, on the other hand, offers the potential to tell stories that make a difference. Little kindnesses add up. When you are your best you, your obituary becomes inspirational.

Some obituaries go into incredible detail about the deceased's work history. Boring. You can do better. As you think about what to include that offers a unique portrait of your life, seriously consider whether anyone will give a crap if you were promoted from one position to another.

It's OK to share what kind of work you did, and where you worked, but those are data points, not life stories. Focus on character, not title, wealth, or position. Share important facts about ethics, values, community service, and helping hands Those are most important. Common people who lead conventional lives have incredible experiences. Capturing memories and sharing them in a meaningful way can make even mundane lives shine like stars.

Think about the times you rose above and beyond your situation and touched lives. Were you involved in any sort of heroic activity? Did you save coworkers who fell through the ice? We'd all enjoy hearing that story. Did you give CPR to a coworker and keep them alive until paramedics showed up?

What effect did that have on you? Maybe you found a flaw in a computer program that saved your company millions? If it's a defining moment for you, include it.

If you're undecided about this section, print out a copy of your resume and stick it here as a placeholder. One day (hopefully before the lights go out) you can come back and decide which details about your work, if any, are most important.

Hobbies

Put the emphasis on your values, not by the time you spent doing things. Titles and big paychecks can't define human beings. You're better than that. Your life is what you accomplished with what God gave you.

Have you been learning to play the guitar for years? Are you still bad? Do you enjoy and appreciate people with guitar talent? Which skills have you mastered, and which ones do you struggle with?

Are you a great cook? Can you sing? Are you skilled at folding napkins or setting a table? Can you write poetry? Your unique talents are important elements of your legacy. What do you love doing? Imagine someone reading your obituary. They're reading it because they are curious. Sharing personal information is what sets your obituary apart. Knowing where you were born doesn't say nearly as much about you as your passions.

Is there a performer or song that always gets you? Music reflects life and says much about our values. When you hear certain compositions are you carried away to far off places? Can you remember the first time you heard your favorite song? Did someone you love share it with you? Did you see an artist in concert, on TV, or hear their song on the radio? Those can connect to life changing events.

Your survivors may have known that you perfected a recipe for French Toast, but they forgot. They may never have known that you could recite the names of each of the fifty states in alphabetically reverse order. What's your hobby, passion, or skill?

Do you love to garden, work with your hands, stand on your head? Did you have the idea for a pet rock long before it came to market? Think for a moment. There's something in your life that involves time and passion. It doesn't matter if you are good at it. It doesn't matter if you never do it in public. Everything you've done or experienced has the potential to become a unique element of your obituary. Remember to put it in context by sharing it as part of a story.

When you write about your hobbies and passions, it may

conjure up other memories of people, places or situations. Those little slices of life help your obituary come to life. Did you pick up a piece of pottery and feel something you'd never felt before? Did your mother take you to a museum where you saw a masterpiece that inspired you to fall in love with painting? Did your grandmother take you to a baseball game? Did you read an inspirational book? Tell the story that surrounds the information.

Great obituaries are entertaining because they tell interesting stories. You've got more material than you might think. Choose examples from activities you'd like to be associated with. Go back to a time before you were interested in a subject that has since become part of the fabric of your life. Explain how your interests came to be. Those things that excite you are essential to a powerful obituary.

Who taught you to fish? Catch a ball? Run? Climb a tree? Hold a yoga pose? You have so many more skills than you normally give yourself credit for. Your life is painted against a colorful background. Don't forget the background.

Reflection

"Interesting people have unusual passions."

Notes

4

Who's Your Soul Mate(s)?

Each of us has a little bit of God that's been there from the beginning of time. I often refer to it as a life spark. Some people call it your soul. Think of it as the spark that comes out of a lighter when you press the trigger. Each time you remember someone who has passed, you're pressing that trigger and releasing their life spark from the darkness.

Life sparks can give us a warm feeling or a shock. They can illuminate rooms or light fires. Sometimes they only produce a spot of light. But every person you have ever known has a life spark. Conscious awareness brings them back into the world. In a sense, that's why making the effort to tell the story of your life is so important. It's a tool your survivors can use to keep you around. And while you're working on your obituary, you are bound to become a better person.

We're constantly experiencing life sparks, but often they go unnoticed. Depending on the time and place, circumstances and our emotional state, life sparks fade away, disappear, or they create a lasting glow. There's more to an obituary than data

47

points and words. Even the most astute philosophers struggle to explain eternity. Mere humans have a hard time understanding what it means to be forever. Keeping your life spark alive in the hearts and minds of loved ones is a metaphor. It's the closest this author can get to explaining life everlasting.

Some people have an effect on us without knowing it. Sometimes we have the same effect on others. On occasion both people feel the connection. Often, one person feels it and the other doesn't notice. As you review your life, try to remember as many life sparks as you can.

That Special Someone

Is your heart an open book? Probably not. We all carry around old flames and unfulfilled dreams. Your obituary is not the place to hurt people with the truth, but there may be an important aspect of your love life that needs explanation.

Romantic love is fleeting. Each of us has felt that light-headed feeling that floats like a butterfly before it stings like a bee. (Cassius Clay wasn't talking about love when he used those words, but they're appropriate in this context.) Writing about the one (or ones) you love is among the more important aspects of your obituary. Then again, after consideration, you might want to skip this section altogether.

The best way to consider the topic is to project what impact your love of another will have on future consumers of your life's story. Love is critical in every life, and messy love is always interesting, but expressing it in an obituary is tricky business. Be careful.

What makes life challenging is that our anticipation usually exceeds the reality of the experience. We long for a storybook love story, but often our expectations are unrealistic.

If you were fortunate enough to experience storybook love, by all means write about it in great detail. If not, express your feelings and move along. My friend Bill married the love of his life. She died long before him, but he visits her grave every day, rain or shine. Bill has many traits that demonstrate impeccable character. His devotion to his wife years after her death paints a clear picture. Most of us yearn for that kind of connection.

It's not news that love is complicated. The emotions and behavior associated with love manifest themselves in different ways. Intimacy, passion, and commitment. And each of those vary in intensity. Over time, love evolves and changes. Sometimes euphoria gives way to anger and jealousy. What kind of love have you experienced? Can you remember the high point? Even if that "head over heels" feeling has faded, try to express your feelings in a rich, meaningful way. Please refrain from tit for tat and cheap shots. We're not perfect, and the people we love are not perfect. Your obituary is a reflection of your life, not a commentary on someone else.

Do you love someone that doesn't know you love them? Does the boy or girl next door (when you were six) hold a special place in your heart? Did you go separate directions and lose track of one another? Want to make someone's day? Tell them in your obituary that they were among the unspoken loves of your life. That's bound to raise some eyebrows.

When you think and write about people you love, be sure to explain why you love them. There are many lessons we learn in love. Do you remember your first love? You don't have to include the story, but remembering that person may help you remember your second love. If there's anyone reading this who can't remember love, take a break and find a quiet place to reflect.

Someone loves you. Even if you don't feel loved right this moment, people love you. Even if they don't act like it, people love you. This is a difficult subject to consider because it's complicated, and because it's always evolving. Someone cared about you deeply, but you brushed them off. Someone wants to love you right now, but you make excuses to push them away.

Love of another requires love of self. Love of self helps us accept those who love us, even when we don't love them the same way.

If you want to skip this section for now, that's OK, but I encourage you to come back and share something about love in your life. Whether you choose to keep it in your final draft is totally up to you, but everyone in your life appreciates being loved and remembered.

Your Best Friend

For some, romantic relationships are not the most important. Maybe when you look back at your life, a specific friendship stands out.

The one who meant the most to you may not even be a person. Those of you who have loved animals could write a book about your pets. That's not the objective here. Instead, let's remember a few special animals and talk about the impact they had on your life. I'm not going to ask a lot of questions in this section. You know their names and their stories. You can choose funny anecdotes or give loving praise to a furry creature who brightened your days.

Write the names of all the pets you had and one thing you remember about each of them. Then pare the list to the one or two that you consider most important. It's the kind of individual twist that will make your obituary something of interest to people who never knew you.

Reflection

"The world will long outlive us, but your obituary ensures you a place in the future."

Notes

5

What Does No One Else Know?

In my second book I mentioned that I lived at a monastery for seven months. Even people who knew me well had no idea I lived with monks. It wasn't a secret; they just didn't know. When you share things about your life that people don't know, it helps us better understand who you are.

We all have things that we've done that are not common knowledge. Some are buried in private corners of our mind, others involve events from our past that aren't secrets, just things we don't often talk about. Your obituary is a good place to dig up and replant some of those seeds. If there are things that people don't know about you, sharing them in the story of your life helps them better understand how you became the person they know.

Was there a pivotal moment in your life? Do you remember what you were thinking and/or feeling when you experienced it? Are there times you'll never forget that you seldom talk about? Did you experience a miracle that you've never been able to explain? Was there a near-death experience?

This is an opportunity to search your memory banks for unusual life events. We all have them. Some were joyous and some were painful. As you explore your past experiences, you'll come across memories that you haven't thought about in years. Maybe you just forgot, or maybe you intentionally buried them. Your obituary is a wonderful place to share deepest remembrances. The day you met your spouse. The day you learned that you have cancer. The day your first child was born. How you learned to ride a bike or drive a car. The day you got your first big job. The day your mother died.

Most of us have experienced things we seldom mention. If that experience helped form your character, set you on a career path, or simply changed the way you look at life, it's worth mentioning in your obituary.

Sometimes we bury childhood memories. Those memories are always with us, but it would be awkward to try to explain them to friends or family. When we are children, we do usual things. Sometimes those long-ago events affect the way we act today. Your obituary is a good place to share explanations for why you are who you are. If you don't share root causes, people may never understand where your ideas or behaviors came from. For example: if you always (or never) do something because of an event in your life, here's a chance to explain. My dad never went to funerals, even for his closest friends. He never explained why, but my guess is his behavior was tied to something he experienced. Do you have "always" and "nevers?" Where did they come from?

Where we get our ideas and behavior patterns is interesting stuff. You may not be comfortable blurting out closely held secrets, but what's the harm of sharing them after you die? "I always wondered why Uncle Buck did that," your niece said aloud after reading your obituary. And now she knows.

Life Lessons

Here's your chance to preach a little. This section is relatively easy. We all make stupid mistakes. (I've made so many I wrote a book about it.) We've all done things we wish we didn't do. We all learn lessons from our missteps.

What's your story? Did you put your finger somewhere it shouldn't have been? Did you drink too much? Smoke? Take stupid chances? Did you hurt someone's feelings with careless words or actions?

Think of this section as an examination of conscience. Allow yourself to recall memories that you've suppressed over time. If this is going to be an impactful obituary, it has to have more than names and dates. Whether you're young or old, you have learned a thing or two during your time on the planet. Here's the section that explains the lessons.

Life is full of curves. We don't always see them coming, and we often react poorly.

If you take chances, you'll occasionally make dumb decisions. That's life. It's not the mistakes we've made, it's the way we owned those mistakes. People who constantly make excuses and blame others seldom improve. When friends and relatives read your obituary, they already know that you weren't perfect. Share something personal that shows them that you benefited from your mistakes.

Even if you didn't make smart decisions during your life, sharing your experience and admitting your mistakes may help others avoid the same behavior. Learning from our bad decisions is what life is all about. Share the experience. Share the lesson.

Most of us have been pissed off more times than we can count. We wish we had controlled our temper better. We've flown into more rages than airports. We've blown our top more than there are active volcanoes on the planet. We often regret our inability to stay calm. After an outburst, we feel remorseful. As we age, our temper explosions are fewer and further between. Sharing temper tantrum stories is revealing.

When you examine your life, are there other aspects of your behavior that you wish weren't there? Bring them front and center in your obituary. When you admit your shortcomings, you will be forgiven. And even if friends and family don't forgive you, at least they'll understand where you were coming from.

In order to find your significant life stories, you need to dig deep. Admitting faults in your obituary will bring more admiration than judgment. To err is human, to forgive is divine. It's our nature to respect and appreciate honesty and authenticity.

Life lessons come in all shapes and sizes. Some are extremely painful. Remembering and sharing them are essential elements of personal evolution. If you can't bring yourself to a complete confession, share what you can. Admitting flaws is cathartic. Human shortcomings are part of your legacy, and we're never too old to ask for forgiveness.

Scars

Physical scars can be distinguishing characteristics. This section of your obituary deals with both physical and emotional scars. How many do you have? What are they? Where did they come from? Do they play a role in your life?

Physical scars are relatively easy to describe and explain. For example: If you had open heart surgery and surgeons split your chest in half, it likely played a role in who you are. For one, there's a zipper down the middle of your chest.

How did you get your scars? What happened? How did they affect you then? How have they affected you since? Is there anything about your scars that people don't know? Some of you have physical scars so small and faded that they are barely visible. And yet, scars are constant reminders of the event that caused them. Emotional scars are generally invisible, but they also linger.

Have you lost a loved one? How has that loss affected you? Have you lived through failed relationships and betrayal? If your feelings are hurt often enough, you develop scars. Those scars manifest themselves in many ways. Most of the angry people we know became angry because of something that happened to them. The same is true for rude and thoughtless behavior. Kind, thoughtful, and empathetic people may have experienced the same sort of event, but they learned a different lesson. In the moment, hurt feelings and rejections feel like the end of the world. With age, we tend to realize that hurt and rejection are a part of life. Negative experiences can either poison our attitude or teach us to be more patient, kind and understanding.

Every broken heart leaves a scar. It's not the size of your

scar that matters, it's the meaning you attach to it. If there's a scar in your life that needs explanation, your obituary is a fine place to sort it out. You can share as many or as few details as you deem critical, but don't leave this stone unturned.

I Wish I Had…

The 2007 movie "The Bucket List" raised awareness of our unlived dreams. For some, it was a game changer. Others of us don't have a bucket list. We never considered making one because we're too busy dealing with the adventures that confront us every day. Some people shy away from their regrets. Regrets have the potential to become a Pandora's box. Before you decide whether to include a section on regrets, consider both the benefits and downsides.

Let's start by making a short list of unaccomplished goals. That should be relatively easy. Do you wish you had learned to fly? Swim? Play an instrument? Take a trip to an exotic location? Run for office? Climb a mountain? Get married? Stay single? What do you wish you had done that you didn't do?

The next part is tougher. If you've already come to grips with your regrets, you're on the road to healing emotional scars that we just examined in the previous section. Great. If you haven't gotten there yet, let's try to put your regrets in perspective.

First, let's sort out your incompletes. If there are more than a couple incompletes on your list, rank them in order of importance. Wish I had…fill in the blank. Hopefully most of those unrealized dreams are about to edit themselves right off the list.

When I hear people say "I always wanted to…" it's usually followed with an acknowledgement that those goals really weren't all that important in the first place. We get in the habit of saying things that don't stand up to rigid examination. When we consider the big picture, most uncompleted wish-list activities are pipe dreams. Making a list helps prioritize and create perspective.

You may have complained for years. "I wish I had done this or that." Most times there are solid reasons you didn't. You may, for example, wish you had moved to another state or country. But when you ask yourself, "What would have happened? Would I have met my spouse? Would I have had children? If I had done the things I "wish I had done," would life be as wonderful as it is?" You've already answered the question.

Most times bucket-list adventures are not as important as we thought. On the other hand, we've all longed for unrealized adventures. That's the intersection of bucket list and regret.

Have you always wanted to see the world from the top of a tall mountain? Walk along the beach of a deserted island? Did you pass up an opportunity that continues to haunt you? Did you miss out on something or somebody because you were afraid to take a chance? All the missed opportunities in life fall under the headings coulda, shoulda, and woulda. That's why serious reflection and focus are critical in this section.

If you have serious regrets and unfulfilled bucket list items, now is the time to fulfill the ones you can. If, on the other hand, those ships have sailed, sharing some of them in your obituary is both healthy for you, and inspirational for future readers.

Now let's consider those other regrets—the ones that aren't so easy to list. Did you shut someone out of your life? Why did you do that? Is there anything that can be done to rectify that situation? Did you have loved ones who died before you could say goodbye? Do you have estranged friends? Family members? Regardless of whose fault it is, have you done everything in your power to heal the divide? These are gut wrenching regrets, the ones that keep us up at night.

There are only two reasons to share regrets: 1. To help you remember so you can do something about it now, before it's too late, and 2. To admit that you screwed up so you can resolve not to repeat your previous poor decisions. Both are solid reasons.

Many of you aren't ready to share those regrets. Even thinking about certain subjects is too painful. That's perfectly understandable. There's a time and place for everything. But if you're going to create a powerful testament, an honest final statement, please consider dredging up even the most unpleasant regrets and exposing them.

Wounds are best covered when they're fresh, but eventually they need air to heal. If you want the full cathartic benefits of an authentic obituary, you'll need to expose some old injuries. If you injured someone and failed to atone at the time, unless it would cause more harm, do it now. If that's not possible, do it here in your obituary.

Missed opportunities are often practical decisions with favorable results. As you go through your list of regrets, try to connect missed opportunities with eventual outcomes. Where were you? What were the circumstances? What did you miss? Why did you miss it? Reviewing a list of missed opportunities is important. What we consider poor decisions are offset by positive results from the decisions we made. In other words, what we remember as a poor decision or missed chance, was really a smart decision that had a positive outcome. Sometimes accomplishments result from what we thought were mistakes. Those stories are always interesting.

There are an infinite number of ways to approach telling your personal story.

The Story of Your Life is a catalyst. A reflective exercise. We cover more subjects than you will include in your obituary. Don't share anything that doesn't feel right or resonate with you. You can approach your obituary in stages. During the first stage, you may pass over some subjects. Then, when your obituary starts taking shape, you can return to them…if the spirit moves you. After you've spent time reflecting, your message will become clearer.

As you dial through your distant past, you'll likely remember weird little things that at first glance you are tempted to poo-poo. Some memories that seem like non-events can, with perspective, turn out to be significant. After reflecting and considering their impact, they may be more important to your story than you originally thought.

Kicking ourselves over missed opportunities is common. We think we turned right when we should have turned left. Chances and people slip through our hands. Why didn't we secure them? We can drive ourselves crazy trying to imagine possible outcomes. But the truth is: we all have to live with our decisions. Some are good, and some could be better. Sometimes we can fix things after the fact. Most times we just need to move on.

As you reflect, try to find overarching themes running through your decisions. Are there obvious patterns? Do you always seem to make poor decisions regarding a particular subject or person? Are there common elements associated with your mistakes and regrets? This section gets to the heart of what makes a great obituary. Digging deep, getting to know and understand yourself is essential. Reflecting about your experiences, leads to honest assessments. Honesty helps create authenticity in your obituary.

Your attitudes about past decisions say a lot about who you are today. Admitting mistakes and coming to terms with regrets, cleanses the soul. As difficult as it may be, presenting the authentic you is your goal. The real you is the only person you want to be remembered.

Once again, whether you include your regrets or not, remembering them is healthy. Time brings perspective. Perspective helps us see things more clearly than we did during the heat of the battle. Everyone has regrets. Sometimes our regrets say more about us than our accomplishments. Future

generations will be grateful that you took time with this powerful element of your obituary.

Quirks and Foibles

Each of us has identifiable behavioral characteristics that distinguish us from others. Do you always put one sock on first? Which superstitions do you practice–stepping over cracks in the pavement, walking around ladders, throwing salt over your shoulder? We all have little quirks and foibles, weird little habits we try to hide from the world. When we think about life, we sometimes only consider the big stuff. We've covered much of that elsewhere, so why not share a couple of your "weird little habits" in your obituary too?

Do you leave one food item on your plate when you finish a meal, or do you always clean your plate? There's a famous football player who turns one of his socks inside out before a game. One famous oil tycoon in Texas was known to crawl around on his hands and knees under his desk when considering major transactions. That wasn't listed in his obituary, but it certainly paints a picture, doesn't it?

Do you have a unique habit? Is there something you always (or never) do? Have people questioned you about the way you do something? Do you, for example, double tie your shoes?

Do you organize the pens or pencils on your desk in a precise order? Do you tap the steering wheel twice for good luck before you start the engine of your car? How about your underwear drawer? Anything unusual there? Do you keep clothes until they are threadbare, or do you toss your wardrobe after one season?

Do you have strange collections? Do you hide things in your house because you like them, knowing that others wouldn't understand? What are they, when did you start the collection, and what do you find special about the things you collect? Do you constantly use a word or phrase that you're fond of?

I had a friend who said, "What the F—?" a half dozen different ways. He always used the same words, but his tone changed depending on whether he was being funny, angry, or confused. At his funeral, after much soul searching, I gave examples of how he used that phrase when I eulogized him. Everyone laughed. It was a strange little foible, but it was his trademark. People in the audience laughed and nodded their agreement. As strange as it sounds, that was his thing, an integral part of his speech pattern. In the midst of our laughter, those of us who loved him felt his presence there in the chapel.

How do you answer when someone asks how you are doing? One of my friends always responded "beautiful." It was a strange answer from a big, burly guy who worked with his hands, but that playful response defined his personality. Do you give unusual answers to common questions? Do you have a sense of humor, or are you literal?

Do you eat popcorn by the handful or one kernel at a time? The little things you say and do distinguish you from others. When you include them, people who know you well will smile. People who didn't know you will gain insight into who you were.

Too often obituaries are bland statements of fact. If you're writing in the third person and you say, "She always ate popcorn one kernel at a time," you've shared something that they'll never forget. Many of the elements of your obituary are serious in nature. It's not a bad idea to break the tension with a few off the wall statements. Favorite foods, things you refused to eat, and anything that you've always done, (or never done) may provide comic relief and create endearing memories.

Reflection

"The richness of life offsets the finality of death."

Notes

6

What Do You Believe?

For many, spiritual life is extremely important. God, family, country, and then everything else, in that order. But today's world is full of skeptics. There are people for whom faith and conviction are foreign concepts from some distant past. The contemporary western world is populated by secular societies where spirituality is neglected and even scorned.

In the future, let's say two hundred years from now, our culture will have evolved in many directions. It's hard to say which religions and faith structures will survive or how they will be practiced. It may be similar to what we know today, but technology and world conditions will surely impact the way people participate in organized religion. In my dreams, I imagine a world where spirituality takes on new meaning for everyone. People pray and live in peace. In my dream, God openly interacts with everyone. Many futurists, on the other hand, predict godless chaos and the end of humanity as we know it. These views represent glass half full and half empty scenarios.

However the world evolves. It's important for each of us

living in this moment to document our values and why we chose and live them. If you are spiritual but not religious, your genetic descendants should know why you chose your path. If you belong to an organized religious group, and it's central to your life, tell us about your faith, why you chose it, and what makes it important for you. Try to articulate for future readers why you feel the way you do about morality, ethics, prayer, and religion. Even if you aren't religious, morality and ethics are core elements of who you are. Try to explain what they mean to you.

Faith and Religion

Most of us believe that there has always been a divine presence in the world. God often surfaces during times of confusion and strife. Religious ideals and practices were often the forces that held societies together. That's not to suggest that all religious people are moral or that people without a spiritual tradition are immoral. Religion is a tool. Some use it to benefit mankind, and some for their own selfish purposes. If you have no interest in religion or spirituality, move on to the next section. No judgment here.

The first book ever printed is the Holy Bible. It has been translated into every language and has the largest distribution of any book in history. The Bible provides guideposts and cornerstones for many of us. If you're a Christian or Jew, there is probably a specific scripture that resonates with you. Including it in your obituary is a simple way to demonstrate your faith. If you've never read the Bible, you might want to take a peek.

There's a reason it's the most read book in the history of the world. Some of the stories seem outdated and weird, but there are also many stories that speak to the same issues that trouble us today.

Whether you attend church regularly or never go to church, here are a few questions to consider in your obituary: Do you believe in God? Do you believe in Jesus Christ, His only son? Do you call God by another name? If you believe in a higher power, but don't consider it God, can you describe that belief? Are you a spiritual person? In other words, do you think about supernatural causes and effects? Has God or religion played an active role in your life? Have you ever experienced something that felt like God's love?

Most people don't wear their faith on their sleeve. Your faith structure is important in your obituary because it explains a lot about the way you live your life, especially the decisions you make. When you are dead and gone, if you don't share your beliefs, people won't understand you. In order to communicate the most complete picture of yourself, your feelings about religion, faith, and matters of the spirit are important. They are part and parcel of who you are.

Did something happen in your life that caused you to believe what you believe? I always tell my children to watch for the signs. In my experience, there are random coincidences in life that can only be described as little miracles. We sometimes call them "God things." You may call them by different names, but we've all experienced situations that defy explanation. Have you seen signs directing you throughout your life?

For example, you think about someone, and then your phone rings and it's them. Is that a coincidence or a little miracle? When you're down on your luck and short a few dollars and a check arrives in the mail for an insurance rebate or escrow overcharge, is that coincidence, or a little miracle? Did you get a strong feeling in your gut to take another route home, only to learn that your regular route was blocked by an accident?

Did you change your schedule before something fortuitous happened as a result? Did you change your routine, and then meet a stranger that enriched your life? When those things happen, do you even consider the cause? Subtle signs abound. What do they mean to you? Including a couple stories about little miracles will give people a better look into your soul. You don't have to be a theologian or philosopher. It's perfectly OK to tell a short story and then explain how it made you feel.

Are you a fatalist who believes nothing matters? Your destiny is predetermined and inevitable, controlled by some undiscovered scientific principles? Do you believe in parallel dimensions with different outcomes? Or do you believe unseen universal forces have a hand in your life? The answers to those and similar questions say a lot about who you are and how you live your life.

Do you believe we have free will? Who is responsible when you choose right or wrong? If you don't believe that God has a hand in your life, what do you believe? Can you articulate it? Whether you believe a little, a lot, or not at all, faith structures play a significant role in every life. Whatever you believe, those beliefs have an impact and deserve a special place in your obituary.

If you pray, pray about how you want to write this section. If you don't pray, spend some quiet time reflecting on the miracles in your own life. Quiet reflection yields answers. Guaranteed.

Politics, Opinions, and World View

The world is full of people who only see it in terms of left and right, liberal and conservative, red and blue. If you're one of them, let it all hang out.

Some people define themselves by political affiliation. We have lived through many historic political events in recent years. All of us have experienced history and seen many history-makers. Context creates interesting stories. If politics is at the core of your existence, this could be your favorite section.

Explain why. Did you touch the emperor's cloak? Were you instantly transformed? In Texas there are thousands who claim to have met President John Kennedy in Ft. Worth the day he was killed. Maybe. For them, the event was a benchmark. Whether they met JFK or not, his death was a milestone. Include the details.

By the same token, politics and politicians are optional. If you don't care about politics, don't include the subject. If you ran for office or played a role in someone's campaign, include a story about the people, places or events associated with that memory. Throughout your obituary, if the story is important to you, share it.

Did you have the opportunity to visit some far corner of the world where you observed cultural differences that changed your opinion about global affairs? Perhaps you took a road trip and came away with a new appreciation for a part of our country that you hadn't seen before. Did you hear a speech by a political figure that forever changed your opinion about an important issue?

Do you believe that all politicians are liars and thieves? Did you tattoo "Build Back Better" or "MAGA" on your buttocks? A little extreme, but if you did, that certainly says more about you than where you went to school.

Worldview and politics are included in the same section in the interest of space even though they're disparate subjects. Which is more important to you? What's your worldview? My neighbor often says, "I hate people." That's his worldview. He really is a nice guy and he treats people with respect, but he prefers being alone to being in a crowd. He values his private time and space, so he tells everyone that he hates people. That way they're not personally offended when he refuses an invitation. How about you?

Looking past politics and political events, do you hold opinions about the world and the people in it? How did you develop those opinions? This section of your obituary could easily evolve into a discussion of your values.

The things you hold close in your heart are certainly worthy of description. Sharing your values and beliefs is a wonderful addition to any obituary. Your story covers both the things people know about you, and things you've never shared before. Your thoughts on unrelated subjects help create "ah ha" moments, elements of surprise. Years from now your words will be even more interesting than they are today.

Few people really know what you believe or how you feel. How could they? Most of us seldom share our deepest feelings. If we don't express them in life, how would they know?

Is what you don't believe more important than what you do? Why do you feel that way? Did someone tell you? Did you wake up one day with a new attitude? When you reflect, can you remember situations and events that sparked specific beliefs?

As you share what you believe, your worldview, try to put it in the context of a story. Give readers some details to help them understand how you came to believe the way you do. Because worldviews evolve, it's important to add context. What did you experience that created your attitudes? Can you surround your attitudes and beliefs with historical context? Even if readers of the future don't agree with what you believe, at least they will have clues about where your opinions came from.

Reflection
"Instead of telling others what to believe,
examine your own beliefs."

Notes

7

What Do You Want to Leave Behind?

How and when we will die is a mystery for the ages. Although we have no immediate plans to die, each of us has a finite number of days on earth. Then what? Old folks often say, "I've lived a good life, and if the good Lord is ready to take me, I'm ready to go." That's healthy. Good for them, right? They're staring death in the face and smiling. Unfortunately, old people aren't the only ones who die.

Young people rarely think about death and when they do, their personal experiences are often incomplete or distorted. Exponential increases in youth suicides and overdoses, school shootings and random acts of violence often dull their attitude about death. They are exposed to the dark side. Instead of developing an appreciation, life and death become conceptual, unreal. Death happens in video games in digital space. TV and movies suck the meaning out of life with so many graphic depictions of death. It becomes devoid of emotion. Life after death becomes a new game or a new player. Death, for many youngsters, is surreal, not worthy of serious consideration.

On top of that, media are dominated by a multi-billion-dollar industry based on fear of death. Pills, forever-young surgery, anti-aging formulas and life-extending gadget ad messages bombard us constantly. Subconsciously we're led to believe that getting old and dying is for losers. We treat aged people like out-of-date products. When people get old, we ship them off to assisted living, far from family. Who wants to look at old decrepit bodies, especially when there are so many beautiful images online? Society is consumed with being forever young.

For some irrational reason, people think they can buy a longer life. Crazy, right? Anyone who is paying attention knows that when your time is up, there's no hiding, death will find you. Refusal to acknowledge aging and death doesn't make them go away.

And there are people who believe we should hasten death. Why wait and grow old when you can snuff it out? That's wrong on every level. I remember reading about a guy who tried to kill himself with a shotgun. He blew off half his face but lived. Ouch. He thought it was the end, but it was the beginning of a painful new life that he never imagined. Not even in his worst nightmare. He counted on sudden death, but it wasn't his time. Blew off his face and lived to tell about it. Well, not exactly tell.

A woman was given four days to live. She required a

double lung transplant. She didn't know where she was on the transplant waiting list. Constant pain led her to consider suicide. And then, in the nick of time, they got the call. After her surgery she confessed the only reason she didn't kill herself was because she didn't want to disappoint her husband who had worked so hard to keep her alive.

Now, perfectly healthy, she breathes with the lungs of a young man who died in an accident. She's alive, and he's dead. If she had killed herself, they'd both be dead.

Life is a series of decisions. Decisions have consequences. The single most guaranteed losing proposition is suicide. It never ends well. My dad used to say, "A person can drown in a glass of water in the middle of a dessert." His way of saying, nobody knows the time or place.

People who think and talk about death have an easier time facing it than those who don't. The less you prepare, the more unpleasant the experience, whether it's you or someone you love. Learning to imagine not being here is transformative. Even though it's a challenge to imagine a world where you don't play an active part, a future where your obituary is all that's left of you, the fact is–we're all headed that direction. You don't need a lecture on death to understand that you're going to die.

We are constantly working to preserve and get the most

from life. Planning for the moment when it's time to let go is not easy. How can you imagine after death when you can't even imagine death? It probably feels a long way off. How can you plan an exit strategy when you're nowhere near ready to go?

Nobody likes death. You don't need to like it to plan for it. For most people that's difficult. It's a real dilemma. We know we're going to die, but we don't want to think about it. Maybe it's easier if you focus on the landscape where your obituary will reside when you're dead.

Here's an example: Imagine your spirit hovering above a funeral home. Friends and relatives are gathered to celebrate your life. Someone close to you begins reading your obituary aloud to the assembled. You're watching their faces. Studying their reactions.

Family members, close friends, and nosey neighbors all gathered to hear what you have to say. What will you tell them?

Now let's imagine a time down the road ten or twenty years later. There's a future audience. People who never met you. Some of them aren't even born yet. They find your obituary and begin thinking about what you have to say. Will your memories inspire unborn generations? What will you leave behind that makes a difference?

There's so much you can accomplish in an obituary. Want

to clear the air? Put someone or something in perspective? Do you need to explain inconsistencies in your behavior? An inaccurate social persona? Do you want to share feelings that are difficult to express? Unspoken apologies? A final word for someone who hurt you? A message of love?

The Truth Is a Powerful Ally

Always keep that in mind. The last thing you want to do is write lies that will haunt you beyond your grave. An authentic obituary allows you to find the peace that comes from spilling the beans. Even if you can't muster the courage to tell the truth in life, set the record straight in your obituary. Telling the truth is guaranteed to lighten your load. And while you're at it, the truth can set you free in other ways. Your obituary may prompt you to make changes in the way you live, the way you love, and the way you process hurt, disappointment, and anger in the here and now. Remembrance and reflection are essential tools for self-improvement.

Clint Eastwood is known to credit the admonition: "Don't let the old man in," for his ability to perform at a high level, even in old age. That's a positive attitude. Nobody benefits from thinking, talking, or acting old.

On the other hand, refusing to acknowledge death doesn't

prolong life. Hiding won't make it go away. Fear of death detracts from the quality of life. "Live like there's no tomorrow," not because we all eventually die, but because life is precious. Make the most of every minute. Celebrate life. Recall and record your memories. Share your joy.

Why should we be afraid? People who are afraid of dying don't take chances. They stay inside and rarely interact with the outside world. If anything, for them, fear hastens death. You don't have to be focused on death all the time, but it doesn't hurt to acknowledge that it's part of your future.

Between now and when you die, there are going to be twists and turns, good and bad. When the good stuff happens, celebrate. When the bad stuff appears, deal with it and move on. No one looks forward to being on life-support. No one wants to be a "vegetable" attached to beeping monitors with tubes up their nose. Nobody would choose to drift in and out of consciousness unable to carry on a conversation. People on life-support never anticipated being there. Bad things happen to good people. But one thing is certain: once you write your own obituary, the bad things won't keep you from sharing your life stories.

Wouldn't it be nice if everyone could die in their sleep? We'd get to a certain age, go to sleep, say good night, and drift away. Most of us hope for that. Unfortunately, many of us will die in hospitals, nursing homes, or with hospice attending us at home. You don't get to choose. Things happen. There isn't a lot we can do about it. By the time we're in the throes of death, it will be too late to make future plans.

So, here's a suggestion: Cultivate a positive attitude about life and death. Enjoy every moment. Take care of essential business now (including your obituary). And deal with everything else as it comes. When you envision a post-death mindset, admitting that it won't last forever, it's easier to concentrate on living the rest of your life. Document what happened so far. Preserve an accurate legacy. Then, when the party's over, you won't be afraid when they turn out the lights.

Reflection

"Consciously live life, and deliberately plan for when it's over."

Notes

Conclusion

Now, Put It All Together

In the days after your death, your friends and relatives are gathered around for a celebration of your life. Someone suggests sharing your obituary. What do you want to say?

Picture the scene from one of the many movies that feature a final reading of someone's last will and testament. People huddled around hoping to cash in on the material wealth of the deceased. In this scenario, it's not about who gets your electric toothbrush as much as who gets your eternal love and gratitude or—if appropriate—your eternal scorn.

Who do you imagine will be most interested in reading your obituary? What message or messages do you want to deliver to them? What sort of tone will you use to deliver those messages? Are you going to shock your audience with details that you haven't shared before? Do you have a special message for readers in the years 2150 or 2249? How will you explain your life to them?

Are you prepared to recall a special memory you only recently thought about? Do you have a special message for your beloved husband or wife? Is there something you're concerned about? A word of caution for the grandchildren? A confession to a neighbor about that dirty trick you played on her? Is it time to set the record straight regarding an old lie?

I hope this book has led you to begin to answer all of these questions and more. But now, it's time for the review and edit stage.

Will you write your obituary and store it in the cloud, or have you decided to use pen and paper? Will you record an audio or video obituary? No matter which you choose, the outline of the previous chapters is a guide to help organize events and memories you wish to share. It's imperative that you open your heart and your memory banks. There's a ton of information in there that you haven't thought about in too long.

Even if you're not totally happy with what you've written or recorded so far, save it. No word, sentence or flubbed recording is a mistake. This is a living document. You can make changes every day. When you're close to the final draft, if you're working on a computer, save it as a PDF. That will help ensure that it remains in the original form. For those of you who don't type, write your obituary in your own hand, lock it somewhere safe, and designate someone you trust to transcribe and post it on the internet following your death.

I'll leave you with some good news and some bad news. The good news is that you've made it this far and you're not dead. The bad news is that there's still work to be done culling and refining your story. Your obituary is a comprehensive accounting of your life, major events, significant people, and deepest held beliefs. Your life doesn't live itself and your obituary doesn't write itself. Now is the time to make decisions and put in a little effort. Unfortunately, there's no guarantee of tomorrow.

Let's review your epitaph. Does it introduce what you've decided to share about your life? Will it capture the attention of future generations? Will your surviving friends and relatives immediately think of you when they read that line? Is it too much? Not enough? You may want to run it by a couple of your closest associates and ask, does this describe me?

Review what you've written about your family. Did you leave anyone out that should be included? Did you tell the world what you think about those family members you included? Will some members of your immediate or extended family be hurt that you failed to mention them? Are there people you consider family who are not blood relatives? Have you included them in this section? Have you sufficiently explained why some people are included and others are excluded? Did you remember to tell those you love that you love them?

For some of us, where we were born says a lot. For others, not so much. What impact does your genealogical geography have on who you are? Do people from your part of the world share unique characteristics? Are you proud of where you came from, or did it create problems for you later in life? Did you stay close to your roots, or have you moved far away? Your physical journey helps tell the story of your life. That journey is different for each of us. Physical location plays a greater role for some, and a lesser role for others.

Do you live where you are likely to die? How did you come to be where you are now? Have you come to a place that resonates? Do you want to stay there until you breathe your last? Do you long to live somewhere other than where you now live? Do you live where you do because of external pressures, climate, family, employment? Those are all interesting facts that help tell your story after you're gone. Where you're from, where you are, and where you want to be might all be the same place, or they could be dramatically different places. These elements help put you in space and time and contribute to an understanding of your story.

Now is the time to expand or contract each chapter. Review the notes that summarize your work experience and consider if they carry the appropriate weight when you think about the sum total of your life. For instance, what, if anything, did you include regarding your career or work? After you've been through this exercise, is your work more or less important than you thought it was? There are no right or wrong answers, but we'll all be interested to know what importance you placed on career and income. For some, it's nearly everything. For others, it really doesn't matter.

As you review the inspirational people in your life, is there anyone you forgot? It's easy to do. Sometimes people who change the direction of our lives get taken for granted. They may be there, day in and day out, making our life richer, and yet when we think about life-changers, we ignore them. Are there people you've never met that changed the way you look at certain things? Did you have a childhood hero, or a distant relative that influenced your trajectory? Was there a doorman or counter clerk at a fast-food restaurant that taught you an unforgettable lesson? Did a stranger say something that stuck?

Have you taken enough time to think back through your life experiences? Have you considered each person that affected the flow of your life? Who you really are, and what you believe. That's the overall goal. There's probably somebody you forgot. We sometimes like to think of ourselves as "self-made" but in truth, each of us is an amalgam of our genetic composition and our collective experiences. You didn't become you in a vacuum. Regardless of how isolated and self-sufficient, you didn't get to where you are without considerable help and influence from others. The ones that had the greatest impact are deserving of special mention in this section of your obituary.

Each day brings new adventures. Every time we interact with other people, every time we're alone, every time something happens, and every time nothing happens, there's a possibility for new adventures and cause for reflection. When we're truly living in the moment, life is full of special events. We can't record them all, but some, especially the recurring ones, are worthy of mention. When our most insignificant thought is weighed against our most important discovery, the scale may not always represent what's most valuable. Little things may mean a lot, and big stuff might not be as important as at first it seemed.

Take another stab at connecting with memories deep down in your subconscious. Did you suffer a traumatic emotional experience? Did your mom leave you waiting at kindergarten? Did your dad spank you for something you didn't do? Was someone else punished for something you did? What were the lessons learned? Did you need professional therapy to resolve internal issues relating to these and other hang-ups? Is that part of your story? Is there value in sharing that experience (for you and others who come after you)?

Don't feel like you need to pour out your soul and all your dirty laundry. It's just that sometimes sharing makes us feel better, and hearing about others' struggles helps put our own in perspective. Whether you're telling your story to get it off your chest, or to teach a lesson to future generations, there's good reason to share more than the *who, what, when,* and *where.* **Why** is the most important question you can answer in your obituary.

As you review your life, ask yourself: "If I was taking a thirty-thousand-foot view of life, what were the game changers?" The people, places, and events that changed the direction of your life are the ones that explain why you are the way you are.

Consider the lessons we should have learned. Since we're all flawed, and we all make mistakes, it's OK to admit shortcomings in your obituary. Instead of making excuses, this is a good time to own them. Unfortunately, most of us have a habit of repeating bad decisions. That makes it hard to admit them. But if you find yourself repeatedly doing things that you wish you didn't, stop doing them. Don't worry about correcting other people, pay attention to your own bad habits and try to break them.

Do you interrupt before someone is finished speaking?

Does your mind wander when you should be paying attention? Is there a distinct separation between your conscious life and your dream life? Sometimes when we get introspective, we go down dark holes and dwell in them. Our sorrows can overcome us. That's not the point.

Reflection is a conscious activity. It's like putting a collar and leash on your memories and taking them out for a walk. When you're finished, you put them away until your next reflective opportunity. It's not something you should do when you're shopping or driving a car. You need a quiet, media-free environment.

Spend time considering your bad habits. Do you eat or drink too much? Rely on drugs to help you make it through the day? Sometimes the key to who we are is hidden (right in front of us) in our bad decisions. Character flaws often go undetected until it's too late to fix them. Those are benefits of self-reflection, remembering, and capturing memories. Your obituary is a perfect communication platform. It's the story of your life.

Ask questions of yourself. Examine your conscience. Honestly consider whether you're everything you could and should be. If you're satisfied with where you are, great. If you feel like making adjustments, start your re-do. It's human nature to cover our flaws and focus on the good stuff, but your obituary should be a legitimate accounting, anchored in truth. Skipping past imperfections violates the spirit of an authentic obituary.

Be bold. Make your life summary comprehensive. Even if you choose not to include all your faults in your obituary, at least be aware of them. Awareness is the first step. If you want to improve your life, take an honest look at who you are right now. Nobody is perfect, but we can try to be a little better each day. If we're moving toward authenticity, we've accomplished a lot, even if we're not there yet.

Your obituary is the essence of your life, preserved forever. You are unique. Every life story is worth saving.

We sometimes need to unwind our life in order to restore and preserve it. If you've answered the questions in the previous chapters, you already know that your story is one of a kind. There will never be another you. Future generations want to know about the past. You are the only one who knows your part of it.

One day technology may automatically preserve memories, but that tool hasn't been invented yet. *The Story of Your Life* preserves your legacy, to be remembered and passed down.

Oral tradition in our world only lasts two generations. If you only "tell" your stories, unfortunately, most of your life will be forgotten. Those stories are worth saving. Now is the time to preserve them in your own words for eternity.

Remembering and reflecting do wonders for our peace of mind. They lower blood pressure, help heal wounds, improve overall health, and brighten even the darkest days.

If you didn't take notes as you read, please go back and start recording your answers. Whatever you come up with, long or short, brilliant or average, will be better than leaving your story to strangers or some AI bot.

Now, get writing.

Notes

Acknowledgements

This book is dedicated to:

John Leonard, my forever friend, who pushes me to write, designs incredible covers, and encourages me when I hit the proverbial wall.

Dan Crissman, the world's finest editor, who understands my thoughts, even those I can't articulate, organizing and compressing them into neat and tidy manuscripts.

Jack LeMenager, whose intellect, attention to detail, and formatting prowess raises my work to new levels.

Jim Babcock, who opened doors, started me on my journey as an author, and delivers constant encouragement.

To God and His Son Jesus Christ, the provider of daily inspiration through whom all things are possible.

And to you. Your reviews provide the fuel that keeps me examining life's challenges. Your questions and comments inspire and direct me. And every time you share my thoughts with a friend, you make my world a better place. Thank you.

About The Author

Charlie Seraphin is an observer of American culture. As a news reporter, radio news anchor, news director, general manager, senior vice president and college professor, he's focused on the important issues of our lifetime. He's personally met and interviewed many of the decision makers that contributed to the stories that shape our world.

In his first book, *One Stupid Mistake*, Charlie set out to explore the complexities of decision-making. He queried hundreds of people about their successes and failures. He is a great listener and meticulous in his attention to detail. He asks probing questions in search of the truth.

While many reporters are focused on macro issues and global politics, Charlie has come to understand that every story begins with an individual decision. What we do, or what we fail to do determines outcomes. How we think, speak, act and fail to act are all reflected in the world around us. People make things happen.

From his early days as a news reporter, Charlie consciously distilled stories into words that everyone can understand. Radio news doesn't work without painted word pictures. He uses plain language and a relatively simple formula. Be fair and respectful. Don't inject opinions unless they're labeled as opinions. Tell memorable stories.

Because voice, tone, choice of words, and many other factors inject themselves into communication, it is foolish to believe in pure objectivity, in journalism or anywhere else. We are all biased based on our environment, background and experiences. Charlie's work is no exception. You'll know where he's coming from and where he stands. But he allows each reader to pursue their individual course of action.

What makes us do the things we do? Why is it so difficult to accept responsibility for what we've done? Heavy stuff, but readers are pleasantly surprised by his wit, humor and common sense. Charlie takes serious subjects and makes them fun and easy to understand.

In *When Did You Stop Being You?,* he explores image projection, especially as it relates to social media, a world of fake personalities and distorted narratives.

Now, in his latest work, *The Story of Your Life,* he brings decision-making and image projection under the microscope of personal reflection, offering an outline for an examination of conscience that forms the foundation for a powerful obituary.

His thought-provoking books challenge us to ask questions, of ourselves and of others. After all, we're all reporters seeking truth. Charlie Seraphin's books aren't intended to provide answers. Instead they help us formulate our own questions so that our decisions are better informed.